T0394777

Blastoff! Readers are carefully developed by literacy experts to build reading stamina and move students toward fluency by combining standards-based content with developmentally appropriate text.

 Level 1 provides the most support through repetition of high-frequency words, light text, predictable sentence patterns, and strong visual support.

 Level 2 offers early readers a bit more challenge through varied sentences, increased text load, and text-supportive special features.

 Level 3 advances early-fluent readers toward fluency through increased text load, less reliance on photos, advancing concepts, longer sentences, and more complex special features.

★ **Blastoff! Universe**

Reading Level

 Grade K

 Grades 1–3

 Grade 4

This edition first published in 2026 by Bellwether Media, Inc.

No part of this publication may be reproduced in whole or in part without written permission of the publisher. For information regarding permission, write to Bellwether Media, Inc., Attention: Permissions Department, 3500 American Blvd W, Suite 150, Bloomington, MN 55431.

Library of Congress Cataloging-in-Publication Data

LC record for Swahili available at: https://lccn.loc.gov/2025018587

Text copyright © 2026 by Bellwether Media, Inc. BLASTOFF! READERS and associated logos are trademarks and/or registered trademarks of Bellwether Media, Inc. Bellwether Media is a division of FlutterBee Education Group.

Editor: Suzane Nguyen   Designer: Andrea Schneider

Printed in the United States of America, North Mankato, MN.

Table of Contents

Jambo!	4
At Home	8
At School	12
After School	16
Usiku Mwema!	20
Glossary	22
To Learn More	23
Index	24

Jambo!

Jambo! I am Juma.
I speak Swahili,
or *Kiswahili*.
Learn some words!

jambo (JAHM-bo) hello

Words to Know

- Kiswahili (key-swah-HEEL-ee) .. Swahili
- jina langu ni (JEE-nah LAHN-goo nee) .... my name is
- ndio (nn-DEE-yo) .... yes
- hapana (ha-PAHN-ah) .... no
- tafadhali (tah-fah-DAH-lee) .... please

5

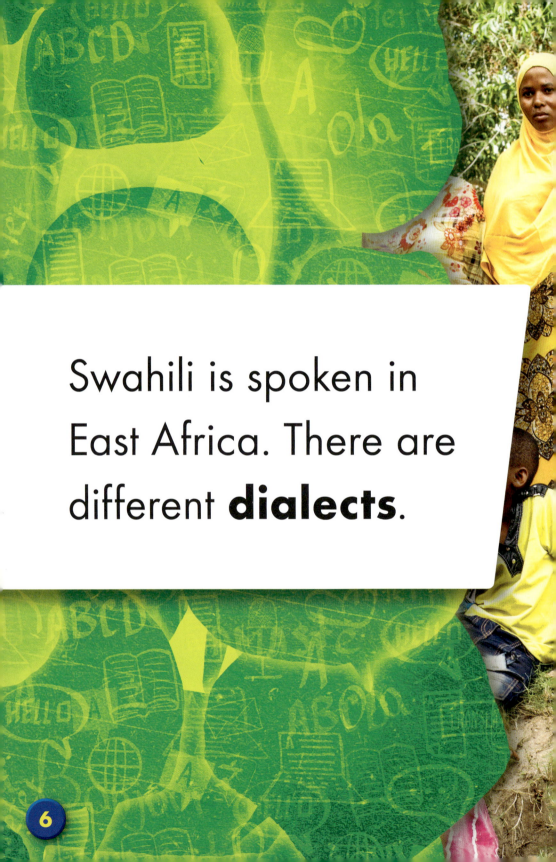

Swahili is spoken in East Africa. There are different **dialects**.

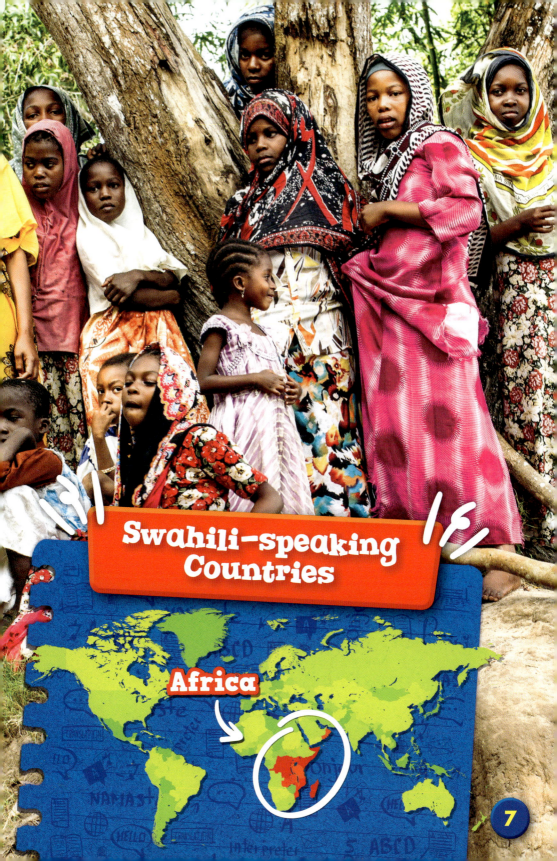

At Home

Adia has a big *familia*. Her *shangazi* and *mjomba* live nearby, too.

familia

Words to Know

- familia (fah-mee-LEE-yah) .... family
- nyumba (NYOOM-bah) .... house
- mama (MAH-mah) .... mother
- baba (BAH-bah) .... father
- kaka (KAH-kah) .... brother
- dada (DAH-dah) .... sister
- shangazi (shahn-GAH-zee) .... aunt
- mjomba (mm-JOHM-bah) .... uncle

9

In the *asubuhi*, Tanga helps his *mama* with chores. He feeds the *kuku*.

kuku

Words to Know

- asubuhi (ah-soo-BOO-hee) .... morning
- kuku (KOO-koo) .... chicken
- anga (AHN-gah) .... sky
- jua (JOO-ah) .... sun

mama

At School

Zuri walks to *shule* with her *binamu*. It is a long walk!

viatu

Words to Know

- shule (SHOO-lay) .... school
- binamu (bee-NAH-moo) .... cousin
- barabara (BAH-rah-BAH-rah) .... road
- viatu (vee-AH-too) .... shoes

binamu

barabara

13

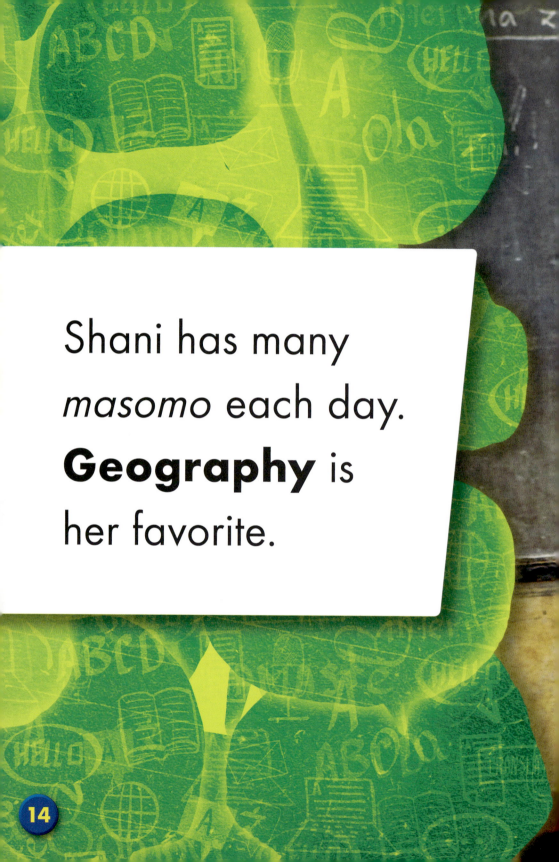

Shani has many *masomo* each day. **Geography** is her favorite.

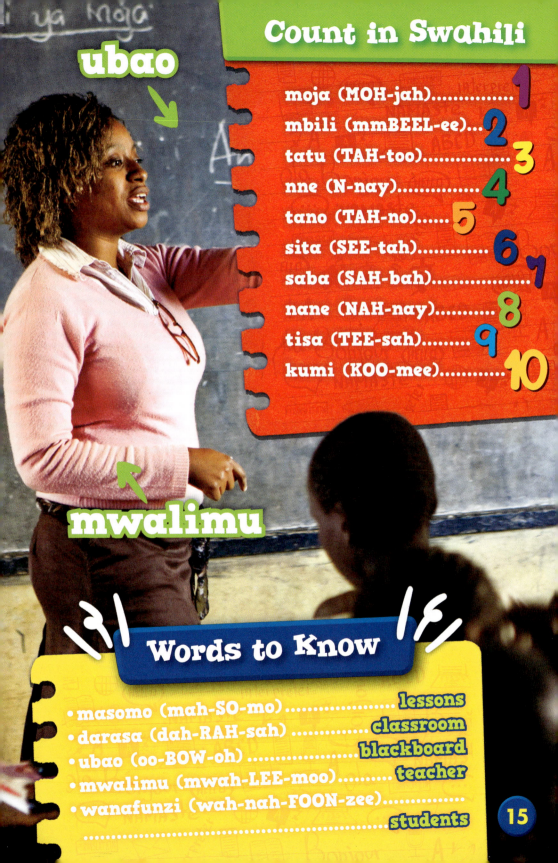

ubao

mwalimu

Count in Swahili

moja (MOH-jah).............. 1
mbili (mmBEEL-ee)... 2
tatu (TAH-too)............... 3
nne (N-nay)................. 4
tano (TAH-no)...... 5
sita (SEE-tah)............. 6
saba (SAH-bah).................. 7
nane (NAH-nay)........... 8
tisa (TEE-sah)......... 9
kumi (KOO-mee)............ 10

Words to Know

- masomo (mah-SO-mo)..................... **lessons**
- darasa (dah-RAH-sah) .... **classroom**
- ubao (oo-BOW-oh) .... **blackboard**
- mwalimu (mwah-LEE-moo).......... **teacher**
- wanafunzi (wah-nah-FOON-zee)................ .... **students**

15

After School

Neema does *kazi za nyumbani*. Then she plays *soka* with her *marafiki*.

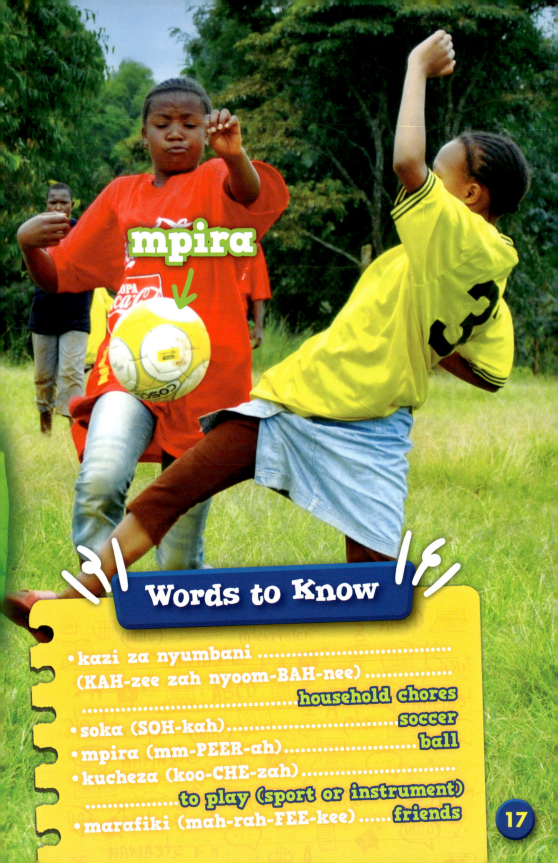

Words to Know

- kazi za nyumbani ....
(KAH-zee zah nyoom-BAH-nee) ....
.... household chores
- soka (SOH-kah) .... soccer
- mpira (mm-PEER-ah) .... ball
- kucheza (koo-CHE-zah) ....
.... to play (sport or instrument)
- marafiki (mah-rah-FEE-kee) ...... friends

17

Faraji's family eats *chajio* together. He uses his *mikono* to eat *ugali*.

mikono

Words to Know

- chajio (cha-JEE-oh) .... dinner
- mikono (mee-KOH-noh) .... hands
- ndizi (n-DEE-zee) .... banana
- ugali (oo-GAH-lee) ...... cornmeal porridge
- maharage (mah-ha-RAH-gay) .... beans
- wali (WAH-lee) .... rice

19

Usiku Mwema!

Mama tells Amani a *hadithi* before bed. *Usiku mwema*!

Glossary

dialects

different ways of speaking one language in different regions

geography

the study of the natural parts of an area on Earth

To Learn More

AT THE LIBRARY

Davies, Monika. *Kenya*. Minneapolis, Minn.: Bellwether Media, 2023.

Golkar, Golriz. *Tanzania*. Minneapolis, Minn.: Bellwether Media, 2023.

S, Goma. *My First Swahili Alphabets Picture Book with English Translations*. AB, Canada: My First Picture Book Inc., 2019.

ON THE WEB

FACTSURFER

Factsurfer.com gives you a safe, fun way to find more information.

1. Go to www.factsurfer.com.

2. Enter "Swahili" into the search box and click 🔍.

3. Select your book cover to see a list of related content.

Index

bed, 20
chores, 10, 16
count in Swahili, 15
dialects, 6
East Africa, 6
eats, 18
family, 8, 10, 20
geography, 14
good night, 21
hello, 5
home, 8
learn, 4
map, 7
plays, 16
school, 12, 14
walks, 12
words to know, 5, 9, 11, 13, 15, 17, 19, 21

The images in this book are reproduced through the courtesy of: Wavebreakmedia, front cover; NIKCOA, p. 3; Ariadne Van Zandbergen/ Alamy Stock Photo, pp. 4-5; Drimafilm, pp. 6-7; Ron Giling/ Alamy Stock Photo, pp. 8-9; Dmytro Titov, p. 10 (kuku); hadynyah/ Getty Images, pp. 10-11; cipariss, p. 12 (viatu); RyanFaas/ Getty Images, pp. 12-13; Andrew Aitchison/ Alamy Stock Photo, pp. 14-15; Diane J Payne, pp. 16-17; Simplice Kaze/ Getty Images, p. 18 (ugali); JohnnyGreig/ Getty Images, pp. 18-19; Ramba/ peopleimages.com, pp. 20-21; Warchi, p. 22 (dialects); 1xpert, p. 22 (geography).